ALL
ABOUT ME

Written by Stephanie Cooper

**NURSERY
WORLD**

TES

NURSERY WORLD
TES

Series Editor Patricia Grogan

Art Editor Lesley Betts
Photography Andy Crawford
Consultant Jo Goodall
Production Lindsay Fogg

First published in Great Britain in 1998 by
Times Supplements Limited

Reprinted in 2000 by TSL Education,
Admiral House, 66–68 East Smithfield, London E1W 1BX

A CIP catalogue record for this book is available from
the British Library

ISBN 1-84122-000-0

Colour reproduction by Create, UK
Printed and bound in Belgium by Proost

Nursery World would like to thank the children and staff
at the following nurseries for taking part in this book:
Beechfield Nursery, London SE6, Greygates Private
Day Nursery, London N10, Sacred Heart Roman
Catholic Primary School, Surrey.

CONTENTS

INTRODUCTION

All About Me contains over 100 activities divided into seven chapters. Each chapter explores one avenue of the book's central theme. The activities are self-contained but also build on from each other, so you can either dip into several chapters when planning your theme or you can use complete chapters. All the activities are firmly underpinned by seven areas of learning to help you incorporate them into your planning. The topic web on pages 8–9 shows you into which areas of learning each activity falls and each activity has symbols representing the areas of learning covered.

Planning a curriculum

The activities in this book are suitable for curriculum planning following all the early years guidelines across the United Kingdom. It is widely accepted that nursery-age children learn best through play and when planning a curriculum it is essential to build child-led play into it. Many of the activities in this book give extension opportunities for this kind of learning but the book should not be seen as a complete curriculum. The book's purpose is to help you build an educationally balanced, varied and exciting curriculum for nursery-age children. Each activity covers one or more of the following areas of learning: Personal and Social Development, Language and Literacy, Mathematical Development, Science and Technology, Time and Place, Physical Development, Creative Development.

Personal and Social Development

This area of learning should have the greatest emphasis in a nursery curriculum. Many of the activities in this book reflect it. The nursery is the stage in all children's lives when they learn how to communicate appropriately with others. This includes sharing, taking turns, showing interest in and playing with other children, making friends, accepting guidance and direction from adults, concentrating and completing tasks, as well as learning how to dress and undress independently and remove and put on shoes. When children are used to the nursery routine, the other children, and when they know the adults they see at nursery areconsistent, positive, and encouraging, they will feel confident enough to develop personally and socially.

Language and Literacy

In this area of learning, children develop their speaking and listening skills, respond to stories, rhymes and poems, look at a variety of books, read books to themselves and others, make up stories, pretend write, write their own names, write using some familiar letters and words and letter sounds, and know that writing has different purposes. Listening to children talk is a crucial element of developing language and literacy. Nursery children are not generally fluent writers but communicate best through speech and gesture. Verbal praise and eye contact encourage children to talk and reveal more about their knowledge and understanding. Children can go to different places and have adventures by reading and writing stories. They can find these imaginative places by reading, and can make them themselves by writing. Whether they are real or pretend doesn't matter. Making marks with paint and chalk is the first step towards learning how to write. Several activities in this book give children opportunities to experiment independently with writing as well as to participate in collaborative writing with an adult acting as scribe. There are also many creative and physical activities aimed at developing fine motor skills to help with emergent writing.

Mathematics

The maths activities in this book aim to make mathematics an enjoyable and fun experience that children look forward to. In this area of learning children develop concepts such as same, different, more, big, little, long, short. They learn how to use common prepositions and phrases such as in, out, on top, underneath, in front, behind, next to. They learn

how to name and recognise colours and how to sort objects by colour, shape and size. Children learn to recognise the following shapes: circle, square, triangle and rectangle. They learn how to count to ten and use number symbols and develop an awareness of number in relation to themselves. By singing number songs and rhymes and copying and describing patterns, children begin using and understanding mathematical language while other areas of learning are also being developed.

Science and Technology

This is an exciting and magical area of learning full of unexpected events which children can witness and react to. Science allows children to become active participants in the learning process. They learn to work as part of a group, sharing equipment and ideas, making predictions and observations by talking about and recording what they see.

Children develop concepts such as hot and cold, wet and dry, hard and soft, clean and dirty, and night and day. They develop an understanding of health-related issues including food, hygiene, and the need for sleep. Children develop an understanding of the weather and other aspects of the natural world. In technology, there is nothing to stop children learning through uninhibited discovery using materials and junk to create their own models, using constructional toys to make a model, or selecting the best materials for a job. Children also discover how to use technology, such as stereo cassette recorders.

Time and Place

This area of learning develops children's language, introducing them to the past tense as they share experiences from their own past. Each time and place activity makes the past relevant to the children by encouraging them to talk about events in their own lives and the lives of others. Looking at artefacts and photographs from their past will hep children to develop a sense of time – before and now. Talking about what happens in the day, and where the children do things will help to develop a sense of place. Activities htat focus on the local environment, facilities and people in their lives will also help develop children's sense of place, and looking at how people live in different parts of the world will develop their cultural awarness.

Creative Development

This area of learning allows children to develop their imagination and to express a response in ways other than by paper and pencil by using and learning how to use a variety of media such as charcoal, chalk, crayon, clay, Playdough, paint, collage, sand and muscial instruments. Fine motor skills are developed to help children with their emergent writing. Children also develop spatial awareness by using shape, colour and form in 2-D and 3-D work. They explore through sound, sight, touch, smell and taste and by talking about stories and songs.

Physical Development

This area of learning covers ways in which children can develop gross motor skills by stretching, jumping, rolling, skipping, running, starting, stopping, balancing, throwing and catching and through imaginative movement. It teaches children to work safely with other children and PE equipment around them. Physical development also concentrates on developing fine motor skills through sewing, painting, drawing, sticking, cutting, and colouring. Activities that promote this area of learning will aid the development of emergent writing in language and literacy and will support many of the aims found in personal and social development by encouraging children to work alongside their peers.

Assessment

There should be an on-going programme of assessment in the nursery which informs nursery staff and parents where a child stands at the time of assessment, and indicates any educational needs. Assessment is a planning tool and should be an integral part of the teaching and learning process. Opportunities for assessment should be identified and included in weekly planning. Assessment should be seen in a positive light informing nursery staff what a child can do rather than what a child cannot do. Without assessment it is impossible to know what learning has taken place. Aims must be clear before the assessment begins. It is useful to have a checklist of expected outcomes with space for comments. The expected outcomes should be kept to a minimum for the observation to be effective. Each activity in this book emphasises more than one area of learning, expressed as a learning outcome. Choose no more than two

to assess at a time, to make the assessment manageable. When carrying out an assessment, the way children are questioned is crucial. Ask open-ended questions to find out what the children are thinking or feeling. The questions should do the following: lead the children to review ideas – why did that happen; promote investigation – which powder will give the cleanest wash; ask children to justify ideas or actions – why; encourage self evaluation – how could you make the ball bounce higher; provide information about children's understanding and misunderstanding – how does it work? At the end of an activity, finished products should be evaluated as soon as possible after they have been produced

so that if anything is unclear you can ask the children about what they have done. Classroom management is vital. The amount of time to be spent observing children must be considered. Children not involved in the assessment must be able to play or work independently or with another adult for this time. Findings should be recorded during or immediately after the observation. Finally, make sure you have a range of assessment strategies and make use of parents' and carers' knowledge of their children in the observation and assessment process.

How to use this book

All About Me is divided into seven self-contained chapters that develop one avenue of the book's central theme. Each chapter has its own coloured bands to help you identify which chapter you are in and its own contents list. The contents list gives you a summary of each activity to help you decide which activities to use. The materials needed for each activity are always found at the top left of the activity and the educational aims are underneath.

Educational symbols

Each activity introduces one or more areas of learning. The symbols show you which areas are covered and the accompanying text gives you the specific aims.

 This symbol shows the activity will develop aspects of language and literacy

 This symbol shows the activity will develop aspects of science and technology

 This symbol shows the activity will develop aspects of creative development

 This symbol shows the activity will develop aspects of mathematics

 This symbol shows the activity will develop aspects of personal and social development

 This symbol shows the activity will develop aspects of physical development

 This symbol shows the activity will develop aspects of time and place

Each activity is numbered for easy reference.

The triangle and circle show you the suggested adult–child ratio for the activity.

Additional symbols

Many activities have additional hints and tips or safety points. They are identified by the symbols shown below.

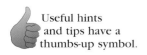 Useful hints and tips have a thumbs-up symbol.

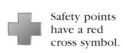 Safety points have a red cross symbol.

Breaking down the information

Each activity either has step-by-step instructions or bullet-pointed instructions under the heading 'What To Do'. Many activities also have suggested questions and extension ideas, also under the appropriate headings.

Topic web

Each activity in this book is underpinned by one or more area of learning. This topic web lists all the activities that develop each area of learning under the appropriate heading. Use this web when planning your curriculum to ensure the activities you use develop all areas of learning according to the particular early years guidelines you are following. This will help you create an educationally exciting and balanced theme that your children will love!

CREATIVE DEVELOPMENT

PERSONAL AND SOCIAL DEVELOPMENT

TIME AND PLACE

SCIENCE AND TECHNOLOGY

PHYSICAL DEVELOPMENT

LANGUAGE AND LITERACY

MATHEMATICS

WHAT DO I LOOK LIKE?

The activities in this chapter help to develop children's understanding of time and place. They enable children to think and talk about their own experiences of the world, bringing to the activities their first-hand knowledge of events and places. There are also many opportunities to create strong links between the children's homes and the nursery – many activities need resources brought in from home, such as family photographs, and some activities need family involvement, too.

Activities in this chapter

1
A book about me
Making personalised books showing each child doing a variety of activities

2
When I was born
Developing awareness of how babies differ from children and how children develop as they grow older

3
What do I look like now?
Exploring growing up by looking at photographs of the children at various ages

4
Birthday song
An alternative to the traditional Happy Birthday song

5
My face
Using a mirror to explore what each child's face looks like, placing emphasis on colour

6
Fingers and toes
Exploring the number 5 by making handprints and footprints

7
When I smile
Using a mirror to study facial expressions and experimenting making marks

8
Different moods
Using exaggerated clown faces to think about feeling happy and sad

9
Looking at my shadow
Step-by-step instructions on how to make a shadow puppet show to see how shadows are cast

10
Body part puzzle
Looking at what our bodies look like and introducing the names of basic body parts by making puzzles

1 A book about me

Materials and preparation

- photographs of the children, including recent photographs, holiday photographs and family photographs
- familiar books
- one homemade book for each child with a photograph of him or her on the front
- glue

 Can talk about places they have visited

 Enjoys pretend writing. Can write own name. Can read a book to self or others

 Can share own experiences. Shows interest in other children

EXTENSION IDEAS

- Leave some of the pages in the book blank and ask the children to fill them in at home with an adult.
- Leave blank books out so that the children can make books during free play, too.

Give the children plenty of time to practise writing their own names.

Questions

- Can you choose some photographs to go inside the book?
- What can we write about the first photograph?
- What other photographs shall we put in the book?
- What shall we write about these photographs?

▶ WHAT TO DO

- Show the children a familiar book and discuss what it contains – pages, pictures, letters and words.
- Show the children the blank books with their photographs on and the photographs they have brought in. Explain that they are going to make a book about themselves.
- Ask the children to write their names on the front of the books. You may need to scribe the name for younger children to follow. Ask the questions below when filling in the books.

Show the children how to stick the photographs into their books without using too much glue.

---

2 When I was born

Materials and preparation

- photographs of the children in different situations when they were babies, for example crawling, eating, laughing
- a photograph of you as a baby
- A2 piece of sugar paper
- glue
- felt-tipped pens

 Can talk about own experiences in the past

 Knows that print runs from left to right in English

EXTENSION IDEAS

- Invite a doctor or midwife into the nursery to talk about babies.
- Invite the parent of a child with a baby sibling into the nursery.

1 Show the children the photograph of you as a baby. Tell them what you looked like, why you cried, what clothes you wore, how you spoke, where you slept, what you played and so on.

2 Ask each child to pick his or her favourite photograph. Stick the photograph onto the sugar paper and ask the questions on the left. Scribe the children's responses.

Questions

- Why is this your favourite photograph?
- What are you doing?
- Is any one else in the photograph? Who?
- What did you look like as a baby?
- Do you look the same now? How have you changed?
- What clothes did you wear?
- What was your hair like?

TIP Let visitors know how long you want them to speak for.

- Ask visitors to bring in relevant objects to show the children, for example hospital name tags and nappies.

What do I look like now?

Materials and preparation

· 4 homemade zigzag books with the pages numbered 0–4 · stick photographs of each child as a baby and aged 1, 2, 3, and 4 years on the appropriate page in each book

Can share own experiences with others. Can talk freely with other children and familiar adults

Can talk about experiences from the past

Shows an awareness of number in relation to self

· Is there a photograph of you aged one in the book?
· When were you two years old?
· How old are you now?
· Show me a photograph of you now.
· Do you look the same now as when you were aged two?
· How have you changed?

▶ WHAT TO DO

Show each child the book containing their photographs and ask the following:
· What did you look like when you were born?
· Show me a photograph of you as a baby.
· What did you look like when you were one year old?

 Ask the more able children to write their own number symbol on to each page.

---

4 Birthday song

NURSERY

Materials and preparation

· birthday cake · appropriate number of candles

Shows awareness of number in relation to self

Can join in with group singing

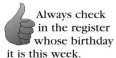
Always check in the register whose birthday it is this week.

Make each child feel special on their birthday by singing this birthday song.

▶ WHAT TO DO

· Light the number of candles to match the birthday child's age.
· Invite the birthday child to stand up in front of the nursery.
· Sing the song. At the end of the song, count up to the birthday child's age with the whole nursery. Clap once for each numbe
· Ask the birthday child to blow out the candles at the end of the activity.

This is Ben's__ birth__day, Ha_ppy birth_day to you Ha_ppy

birth_day to you Ha_ppy birth_day to you This is Ben's_

birth__day, Ha_ppy birth_day ha_ppy birth__day to you

My face

This activity helps children develop their observational skills.

Materials

small mirrors · paper · coloured pencils · felt tipped pens

 Can make a mark using a paintbrush.

 Explores colour in 2-D

 Respects other cultures

 Names colours. Uses number in relation to self

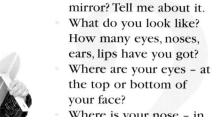

1 Give each child a mirror and ask them to study their faces. Ask them the questions on the right.

- What can you see in the mirror? Tell me about it.
- What do you look like? How many eyes, noses, ears, lips have you got?
- Where are your eyes – at the top or bottom of your face?
- Where is your nose – in the top or middle of your face?
- What else can you see on your face?
- What colours can you see on your face? Give the children plenty of time to think about the colours they can see.

EXTENSION IDEAS

- Introduce the more able children to pictographs.
- Ask the children to find out the colour of everyone's eyes. Scribe a list for them.
- Let the children cut eye shapes out of white paper and colour in the shapes according to the list of eye colours.
- Make the pictograph with the children.

JULIANNE.

2 Show the children the materials on the table and ask them to make a face that looks like their own.

3 Encourage the children to think about the colours on their faces as they draw.

 Introduce yarns of coloured wool. Ask the children to add hair to their pictures using the coloured wool.

Fingers and toes

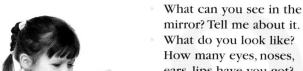

Materials and preparation

· plenty of newspaper · bowls of mixed powder paints · paper for printing · bowls of warm water · paper towels · lay the newspaper on the floor and table, pour the paint into shallow bowls that the children can step into

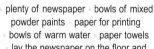 Can put on and take off shoes and socks

 Can count to 5

 Can open fingers

 Explores properties of paint

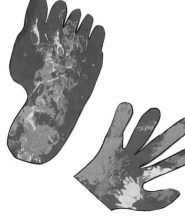

This is a fun, but messy activity. Keep a supply of paper towels near the bowls of warm water to dry off the children's feet after washing them.

1 Tell the children to take off their shoes and socks. Ask them to count their toes. Ask how many they have on one foot. Do the same with their fingers.

2 Ask the children how they might make footprints on the paper. Let the children experiment making footprints. Now ask them to make handprints.

When I smile

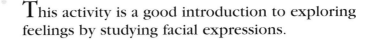

Materials and preparation

- paper · coloured crayons
- felt tipped pens · small mirrors

 Can participate in a group activity led by an adult

 Can control pastels to make a mark on paper

 Can talk about different feelings to the group

This activity is a good introduction to exploring feelings by studying facial expressions.

1 Give each child a mirror. Ask them to study their faces in the mirrors when they are smiling. Ask them to draw their smiling faces.

2 Repeat the activity asking the children to pull sad, surprised and cross faces.

Questions

- What makes you smile?
- Can you smile now?
- What happens to your face when you smile?
- Do you see extra lines on your face? Where? Why do you think this happens?
- Can you see more of your teeth?
- Do your eyes get bigger or smaller?
- What happens to your lips, cheeks?

8

Different moods

Materials and preparation

- pictures of people looking sad and people looking happy
- face paints
- drawings of happy and sad clowns

 Can participate in a group activity led by an adult

 Can talk freely about own experiences

This activity can be used as an extension to When I smile (7) page 14.

1 Ask the children what makes them happy or sad. Show them the pictures and ask the questions on the right.

Questions

- Which pictures show sad people?
- How can you tell they are sad?
- Why do you think they are sad?
- What happens to your face when you are sad?
- Have you cried before?
- What happened to your eyes when you cried?
- Ask the above questions about the happy pictures.
- What happens to your lips, cheeks?

EXTENSION IDEAS

- Ask the children to describe happy and sad events. Scribe their responses into a homemade book.
- Sing 'If you're happy and you know it, clap your hands'.
- Make papier mâché clown faces with different expressions
- Talk about different emotions.

2 Copy the clown templates on page 63. Use them as a guide to paint happy and sad clown faces on the children. Talk about the exaggerated features, and ask the children to role play why they may feel happy or sad.

Looking at my shadow

Materials and preparation

overhead projector or lamp with a strong light · thin card · scissors · paper fasteners · tape · gauze to make a screen for the shadow puppets

 Uses appropriate language to talk about size

 Can make shadows

This activity can culminate in presenting a show to the children's families.

1 Show the children how to cast shadows on the wall using the overhead projector or the lamp. Talk about how the shadows are made and the importance of light.

Questions

· What does your shadow look like?
· Can you make other shapes?
· How do you think the shadows are made?
· What do you think happens to the light?

Shine light behind a gauze screen and hold the puppets in front of the screen.

2 Enlarge and cut out the shadow puppet templates on page 62.

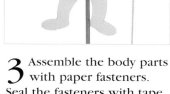

3 Assemble the body parts with paper fasteners. Seal the fasteners with tape.

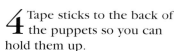

4 Tape sticks to the back of the puppets so you can hold them up.

Body part puzzle

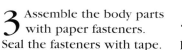

Materials and preparation

card · scissors · coloured pencils · sticky-backed plastic

This activity introduces children to the names of basic body parts.

 To fit together a simple fit together jigsaw

▶ **WHAT TO DO**

· Follow the step-by-step instructions for how to make the puzzle.
· Show the puzzle to the children and ask them to name the parts – head, arms, legs, hands, feet and so on.
· Talk about the parts of the body and what they do.
· Leave the puzzle out for children to do during free-play times.

1 Enlarge and cut out the body template on page 62.

2 Colour in the body and cover it with sticky-backed plastic.

3 Cut the puzzle into five pieces and ask the children to make the puzzle.

ALL ABOUT MY FAMILY

The activities in this chapter will help children to learn about families. The children will develop an understanding of their role in their own families and will learn about different kinds of family. Some of the activities focus on family members who live far away. These activities are ideal for involving parents in multicultural nurseries and will also help children to understand and respect other cultures. Always ensure you are aware of each child's home environment and adapt activities where necessary.

Activities in this chapter

1
My family
A book-making and discussion activity encouraging children to think about their families

2
At home with my family
Encouraging children to think about family routines and the time they spend at home

3
Family occasions
A discussion activity focusing on family occasions

4
Visiting my family
An extension activity to My family (1) page 17 where the children develop an awareness of family members who don't live with them

5
Letter writing
Thinking about family members who live far away and how children can keep in touch by writing to them

6
Posting letters
An extension activity to Letter writing (5) page 19 where the children help an adult scribe and address a letter

7
Another family
Examining other kinds of family by reading the story "The Three Little Pigs" and making junk houses

8
Our nursery family
Comparing the heights of everyone in the nursery and making a collage to show everyone's height

9
Visitors
Learning the difference between family members and visitors and how to use a camera

10
Flats and houses
Developing an awareness of the different kinds of home that families live in

11
The numbers in our street
Encouraging children to think about their home and its place in their neighbourhood

12
My neighbourhood
Developing awareness of the facilities the children and their families use, including shops, public transport, and doctors' surgeries

13
Families that live far away
Focusing on family members who live in another country

14
Flags and patterns
An extension to Families that live far away (13) page 23 making country flags and studying their patterns

My family

Can talk about their own families

Can share own experiences with others.

Can speak clearly. Talks freely

EXTENSION IDEAS

• Leave some of the pages in the book blank and ask the children to fill them in at home with an adult. You could then discuss what they did the next day.
• Leave blank books out so that the children can make books during free play, too.

Show the children the books and family photographs. Ask them to tell you about their families using the questions on the right.

Let the more-able children stick their photographs in the books themselves.

If children don't have many family photographs, ask them to paint pictures of their family.

Questions

• Who lives in your home?
• Do some of your family live somewhere else? Where? Tell me about them.
• Does anyone have a brother/sister? Is he/she older or younger than you? Tell me about him/her.
• Who has grandparents? Tell me about them.
• Does anyone have a pet? Tell me about it.

At home with my family

Can talk freely with adults and children. Can participate in questions and answer sessions

Shows interest in familiar adults. Participates in group activities led by an adult. Can share own experiences with others. Can take turns

Mummy painting at home

Daddy sanding the walls at home.

▶ WHAT TO DO

• Stick the photographs in the book and show them to the children.
• Ask the children to think about all the things they do at home with their families.
• Talk about daily routines, such as meal times and bedtime.
• Ask the children to draw crayon pictures of themselves doing things at home.
• Stick the pictures into the homemade book.
• Ask the children to describe their pictures and scribe their answers.

Family occasions

Materials and preparation

An item relevant to the occasion you want to talk about, such as a bridesmaid's dress, or an invitation to a special occasion such as a bar mitzvah

 Can talk freely with other children and familiar adults

 Shows interest in the experiences of others

EXTENSION IDEAS

- Make a class book called Special Family Times.
- Ask the children to think about a special occasion to draw and write about in the book.
- Occasions chosen could include an uncle getting married and a mother's birthday.

This activity can be developed throughout the year.

Say 'I need you to listen carefully, then you can touch the dress'. This will get the attention of all the children.

▶ **WHAT TO DO**

- Tell the children you have brought in something special that you want to show them. Explain the object is fragile and delicate, so needs to be handled carefully.
- Ask the questions below.

Questions

- What do you think it is?
- Who do you think wore it?
- What do you think it is made of?
- Have you seen anything like this before? Where? What was happening when you saw it?

Visiting my family

Materials and preparation

· homemade books containing family photographs · marker pens · A3 piece of paper

 Shows interest in familiar adults. Can participate in a group activity. Can take turns

 Knows that words have meaning

 Can talk about own family

Differentiation

- For more able children, ask, 'Can you draw a picture of how to get to your grandma's house? Can you help me write down the directions to get to your uncle's house?' Talk about friends who live nearby, too.

This activity can be done as a follow-up to My family (1) page 17 – you could use the books made in this activity, too.

▶ **WHAT TO DO**

- Tell the children about a relative who lives far away – in either this country or abroad.
- Ask the children if they have any relatives who live far away. If there are photographs of the relatives in the homemade books from My family (1) ask the children to point them out.
- Give the children time to talk about their relatives, who they are and where they live.
- Ask the children if they have visited their relatives. If so, how did they travel there?

Use maps and globes to show the children where their relatives live.

Letter writing

Materials and preparation

• sack of letters of different sizes addressed to different people • a favourite post story • large piece of sugar paper • marker pen • writing paper with your nursery's name written at the top • envelopes • old stamps

 Can participate in group activities led by an adult

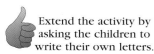 Can listen and respond to a story. Can recognise familiar written words. Shows an awareness of some letter sounds. Can write familiar letters. Understands that writing has different purposes

Extend the activity by asking the children to write their own letters.

1 Ask the children to pick out letters from the sack. Ask them to work out to whom the letters are being sent and what they are about.

Uncle Andrew
12 Shrewsbury Road
Potters Green
Liverpool
LL7 8AU

1st

2 Ask the children to help you write a letter. Write on the sugar paper and ask the questions on the right. Put the letter into an envelope and show the children how to address the envelope.

▶ WHAT TO DO

• Read a favourite post story, such as 'The Jolly Postman' by Janet and Allan Ahlberg, Heinemann.

Questions

• Who shall we write to?
• How shall we start?
• What do we want to say?
• Do we want to ask anything? What?
• Do we want to tell the person anything? What?
• Is there any special news we can write about?
• What shall we write next?
• How shall we finish our letter?
• What shall we write on the envelope?
• Where shall we put the stamp? Why do we need a stamp?
• Where can we post our letter?

6 Posting letters

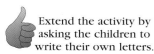 Enjoys listening to poems

This activity is a follow-up activity to Letter writing (5) page 19.

The pillar box is
fat and red.
Its mouth is
very wide.
I'm going to
take some letters
And pop them
all inside.
1, 2, 3 ...

▶ WHAT TO DO

• Teach the children the poem and say it out loud.
• Ask 'how many letters did we post today?
• Who did you write to?
• What did you write?
• Did you write to somebody in your family, to a friend, or somebody in a story?'

EXTENSION IDEAS

• Invite a postperson in to the nursery, or arrange to visit your local post office.
• Make a post box into which the children can post letters.
• Organise the children into supervised groups to post letters in a post box.

Another family

Materials

- a selection of junk and card
- brown, black and yellow paint
- paint brushes • sponges for sponge printing • art straws • plastic straws
- scissors • masking tape • glue
- straw • small sticks

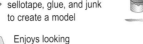
Can use scissors, sellotape, glue, and junk to create a model

Can talk about stories. Explores the properties of paint

Enjoys looking at books

Questions

- How can we use the things on the table to make a model of one of the houses in the story?
- How can we make it look as though it is made from straw?/bricks?/sticks?
- What shape will you make your house?
- What colour will your house be? Why?
- How will you make the windows and the door? Will they open? How?
- How will you make the chimney?
- How will you join the junk together to make your house?

▶ WHAT TO DO

- Read the traditional story 'The Three Little Pigs'.
- Tell the children they are going to make their own houses with the materials listed in the materials box. Base the houses on the pig's houses in the story.
  Ask for whom they want to make the house – their own family, a family in a story, their nursery family and so on.
- Ask the questions on the left.
- Ask the children to make 3-D houses using the junk materials.
- Make a display with the junk houses.

Let the children talk for as long as they want – they are giving you a verbal plan.

Our nursery family

Materials and preparation

- wall space for measuring the children's height • paper stuck to the wall • pencils

Shows an interest in other children. Can follow simple instructions

Can recognise own name

Can control a pencil to draw a face with features

Shows an understanding of taller than and shorter than

You could compare any of the children's features to help them think of themselves as a group.

▶ WHAT TO DO

- Choose two children, one taller than the other. Ask who is the tallest/ shortest?
- Ask the children how they could compare all their heights. Listen carefully to their answers and then suggest measuring them against the wall.
  Measure each child in turn by drawing their outline on the paper. Put the child's name next to his or her outline.

Repeat this activity every few months to show the children how quickly they grow.

Materials and preparation

camera with film • homemade visitors' book • a used visitors' book to show as an example • marker pen • photographs of recent nursery visitors

Writing for different purposes. Enjoys looking at books

Shows interest in familiar adults

Refer to the visitors' book regularly, so the children are reminded of its purpose.

Talk to the children about unwanted visitors, too and why they should always ask an adult to answer the door to visitors.

Visitor's book

1 Show the children a used visitors' book and ask the questions on the right.

Extend the activity by asking the children to write to their most recent visitor.

2 Show the children how to use a camera and let them take photographs of future visitors for the book.

Our parents visited us on our nursery Sports Day.

3 Stick in the photographs of the visitors in the book and scribe the children's comments about the visitors.

Questions

- Does anybody get visitors at home? Who is a visitor?
- Does anyone have a visitors' book? What is a visitor's book?

Materials and preparation

Selection of pictures showing houses, flats, bungalows, tents, caravans and so on on a table

Can initiate ideas

Can talk about where they live

Uses appropriate language to describe shape and size. Can sort pictures

Extend the activity by talking about different cultures and how they live.

This discussion activity will help children realise that people live in all kinds of homes.

Questions

- What can you see on the table?
- What kinds of home can you see?
- Who do you think lives in these homes?
- Could all your family fit into the tent/hut and so on?
- Tell me about where your family live. What do you live in? What does it look like?
- Can you sort the pictures into kinds of home, for example houses and flats?
- Are there any shapes in the pictures? Which ones? What shape are the windows? The doors?

The numbers in our street

Materials and preparation

• brown, grey, black and green powder paints • sponges for sponge printing • selection of junk material • scissors • sticky tape • pictures of different kinds of home • pretend road scene

 Can use junk to create a model

 Can talk about where they live

 Can count to 10. Can recognise number symbols to 10

 Can join in group activities led by an adult

 Add street names and sign posts to the road scene.

This can form a follow up activity to Flats and houses (10) page 21.

▶ WHAT TO DO

• Talk to the children about different kinds of home and ask them to tell you about the buildings near their homes and the nursery.
• Show the children the pretend road and ask them to make junk buildings to go on the road. Use the pictures from Flats and houses (10) for reference.

Questions

• Can you tell me about the street or road where you and your family live? What does it look like? What is on the road? Are there just houses or other buildings, too? What are the other buildings? Are there any really tall buildings on your street or road?
• Can you make some model buildings to go on our pretend road?
• What shape will you make your building? How will you make the doors, windows, chimney and so on?
• Where shall we put the model buildings on the road?
• How shall we number the buildings? Which number should come first?
• How many buildings are in our street?

My neighbourhood

Materials and preparation

• pretend road scene • selection of toy cars, buses, trains and so on • pictures of typical amenities such as shops, doctor's surgery, chemist, playground and so on

This activity makes children think about the people and amenities their families need.

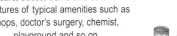 Explores properties of paint

 Can join in a group activity led by an adult

 Can use junk to create a model

▶ WHAT TO DO

• Show the children the pretend road scene and as them to tell you about what they can see on it.
• Talk about any amenities they can see on the road scene and which amenitie they think are useful. Ask the questions on the left.
• Talk about the transport ir their neighbourhood. Ask the children to role play typical journeys around their neighbourhood.
• Leave the road scene and toys out so the children can continue role playing during free-play time.

Questions

• What things do your family need to have near their home?
• Why do we need shops?
• Why do we need a doctors' surgery?
• Why do we need a dental surgery?
• What else do we need?

Families that live far away

Materials and preparation

- flour · olive oil · jug of water
- creamed tomatoes · topping ingredients
- mixing bowl · baking sheet

Uses mathematical language to talk about measure, colour and shape

Families and where they live

Understands the need for hygiene when handling food

Can participate in group activities led by an adult. Can take turns. Can concentrate for a reasonable length of time

Let the children take turns mixing the dough.

Adapt this activity according to the nationalities of children in your nursery and invite parents in to help, too. This activity is ideal for children with Italian relatives.

1 Tell the children you are going to have an Italy day for relatives who live in Italy. Show them the pizza ingredients.

2 Add 2 tablespoons of olive oil to 250g of flour in the mixing bowl. Add water one drop at a time and mix into a ball of dough.

3 Let the children choose the ingredients for the topping and put them on the pizza base.

4 Cook the pizza in a fairly hot oven for 20 minutes, until the base is golden brown and the topping is crispy.

Differentiation

- Ask more-able children what they think happens to the water when it is added to the flour.
- Ask more-able children to measure the ingredients for you.
- To save time with younger children, you could use ready-made pizza bases instead.

Make sure you are aware of any dietary restrictions before doing any cooking activity.

Take care when using a cooker. Ensure it is checked regularly by a health and safety inspector.

Flags and patterns

Materials and preparation

A painting of an Italian flag
- powder paints in a variety of colours
- paper · paintings of flags from other countries

Can name shapes and colours

Can make marks using a paintbrush

Families and where they live

For more-able children, extend the activity to talk about shapes and patterns in a variety of flags.

Make flags as an extension activity to Families that live far away (13) page 23.

▶ WHAT TO DO

- Paint the relevant country flag.
- Show the children the flag and ask them to paint their own flags.
- Ask how many colours and what patterns there are on the flag.
- Show the children the pictures of the other flags and ask them to choose another flag to paint. Talk about the country each flag represents.

Use globes and maps to show where the different countries are.

WHAT CAN I DO?

This chapter is packed with activities that heighten children's awareness of how much they can do, and give you opportunities to reinforce what the children are good at. Many of the activities concentrate on physical development. Warming up for physical activities is very important. Activity 8 on page 28 gives you useful warm-up ideas. Warming up helps to loosen joints and muscles and prepares the children for all the stretching, jumping and running they'll be doing. When the children are doing physical activities, always offer lots of praise and encouragement particularly for original ideas, or if someone is working safely.

Activities in this chapter

1
I can sing
Learning the words and actions for a popular song and making up new verses

2
Action song
Learning the words and action for 'Heads, shoulders, knees and toes' and trying to keep a tune when words are taken away

3
I can play
A fun version of the game tag to encourage children to participate in group activities

4
I can sew
An introduction to sewing techniques that will help develop hand–eye coordination and fine motor skills

5
I can paint
A creative activity that encourages children to explore all sorts of painting techniques

6
I can describe and listen
Listening and describing pictures to develop concentration skills

7
I can cook
Making scones to share as a group in the nursery. Mathematical language is developed in this activity

8
I can stretch
Fun warming-up activities to prepare children for physical activities

9
I can throw and catch
Group and solo exercises that help to develop children's hand-eye coordination

10
I can slide
Exercises that develop children's gross motor skills and encourage them to work alongside each other safely

I can sing

  Listens and responds to songs

Enjoys singing and joins in with others

1.The wheels on the bus go round and round,

Round and round, round and round. The

wheels on the bus go round and round.

All day long._____

If the children are unable to make up a whole verse, prompt them with the beginning of an idea such as, the grandmas on the bus go. Then, ask the children to finish the verse.

▶ **WHAT TO DO**

- Teach the children the tune to the song
- Follow steps one to four for the words
- Ask the children to make up their own actions.

1 The wheels of the bus go round and round

2 The mummies on the bus go nod nod nod

3 The babies on the bus go waa waa waa

4 The daddies on the bus go chatter chatter chatter

Action song

 Listens and responds to songs

 Enjoys singing and joins in with others

Head shoul_ders knees and toes, knees and toes,

Head shoul_ders knees and toes, knees and toes_ and_

eyes and ears and mouth_ and_ nose

Head shoul_ders knees and toes, knees and toes,

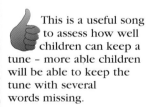
This is a useful song to assess how well children can keep a tune – more able children will be able to keep the tune with several words missing.

▶ **WHAT TO DO**

- Teach the children the tune and actions to the song – touching each part of the body as it is sung.
- When the children are confident with the words and actions, start missing words out but keep the actions.

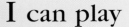

3   I can play

 Can play alongside other children. Can take turns. Can participate in group activities led by an adult

 Can run around a circle. Can sit still, sit down and stand up

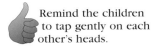 Speech is clear. Listens when others are speaking

Remind the children to tap gently on each other's heads.

Make sure the children are in bare feet or wearing shoes that are safe to run in. Ensure the floor is free of splinters and so on.

Make sure you have lots of room for this activity and limit the group size so the activity does not become too boisterous!

▶ WHAT TO DO

- Choose one child to be 'it'.
  That child walks around the circle tapping each child gently on the head saying 'duck, duck' as she goes.
- When she touches a child and says 'goose' the running starts.
- The goose has to catch the child who is 'it'. They must stay on the outside of the circle and must keep running the same way. The 'it' child is safe if she can make it to the goose's place in the circle without being caught.
- Then the goose is 'it'.
- If the goose catches her, she is it again.
- Then it all starts again ... 'duck, duck, duck ...'

4   I can sew

Materials and preparation

- beads which will thread on to a shoelace • A5 card with holes around the edge or along the middle (use a hole punch to make the holes where you want them) • ribbon • coloured wool • scissors • felt in various colours • large needles suitable for the children to use

 Can thread beads onto a shoelace

 Explores card, ribbon, wool and felt

Sewing With Shapes

1 Show the group how to thread beads on to the shoelace. Let the children have a go, then show them how them how to do running stictch on the card.

2 Explain that you are going to do some sewing today. Show the children the items on the table and let them experiment sewing.

 Always have an adult present when children are using needles.

TIPS Show the children different ways of sewing, such as up and down and in wobbly line.
- As the group are sewing, ask what they are making and how. Only help them if they are struggling.
- As an extension activity, show the children how to turn corners and make their own placemats with felt.

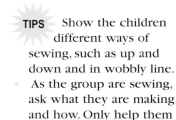

I can paint

Can talk about pictures. Explores paint, sand, sawdust and glue

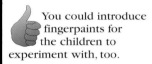
Can take reasonable care with equipment

Can control a paintbrush, sponge rollers and sponges to make marks

Check for allergies before introducing the sawdust.

You could introduce fingerpaints for the children to experiment with, too.

This activity can be extended to include model making and drawing, too.

1 Lay the materials on the table and let the children experiment painting anyway they like.

2 Ask what they have painted and how and why they used the materials they have.

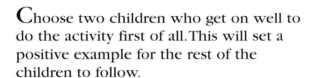

3 Mix some sand and paint and some sawdust and paint and let the children experiment with the textures.

4 Show the children how to do sponge painting and let them experiment with this technique.

I can describe and listen

Choose two children who get on well to do the activity first of all. This will set a positive example for the rest of the children to follow.

Can follow simple instructions

Speaks clearly

▶ WHAT TO DO

- Give the describing child the coloured-in picture and the listening child the plain picture.
- Ask the describing child to hold the picture so the other child cannot see it and then describe it.
- Ask the listening child to colour in the picture exactly as the describing child describes it.

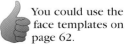
You could use the face templates on page 62.

I can cook

Materials and preparation

- 225g self-raising flour · 40g castor sugar · 75g butter · 50g dried fruit · 1 beaten egg · 4 tablespoons milk · greased baking tray · mixing bowl · wooden spoon · weighing scales · sieve · rolling pin · pastry cutter

Can participate in a group activity led by an adult. Can take turns. Can concentrate for a reasonable length of time

Uses mathematical language to describe measure, colour and shape

Understands the importance of hygiene when handling food

1 Add the butter and sugar to the sieved flour. Crumble the ingredients to a bread-crumb consistency.

2 Add the beaten egg, milk and fruit. Mix the ingredients to make a dough. Add flour as necessary.

3 Roll out the dough to a thickness of 1 cm on a floured surface. Cut the dough with the pastry cutter.

4 Transfer the scones to the baking tray. Bake at 220°C, 425°F, Gas mark 7 for 10 minutes until golden brown.

▶ WHAT TO DO

- Tell the group you are going to work together to make some scones.
- Ask if anyone has made scones before and how they made them.
- Show the group the ingredients and ask what they are.
- Ask the children to help you measure out the ingredients and talk about the weights and measures.
- Follow steps one to four to make the scones.
- Make sure each child has a turn at adding ingredients, mixing and rolling out.

✚ Ensure the children know to keep away from the hot oven.

8

I can stretch

Can make a fist. Can open and close fingers. Can run, changing direction, with control. Can jump with feet together. Can balance on one leg. Can stretch up and reach down

Use these exercises to warm up children ready for more strenuous activities.

Move quickly from one activity to the next so the children are warmed up as well as loosened up.

▶ WHAT TO DO

Tell the children to take off their shoes and socks and do the following:
- Wiggle your fingers.
- Make a fist, open and close your fingers.
- Shake your hands/feet – make your wrists/ankles do all the work.
- Wobble your arms – make your shoulders do all the work.
- Draw a circle with your finger/right arm/left arm/right leg/left leg.
- Stretch up high – stretch everything, arms, legs, fingers, toes, neck.
- Bend down, jump up after 5 – 1, 2, 3, 4, 5 Blast off!
- Jog/skip/jump/walk/ tiptoe/take giant steps around the room for one minute.

I can throw and catch

Materials and preparation

bean bags · cones · small rubber rings · small balls · large balls · rope to tie around two chairs and stretch taut

Can play purposefully alongside other children. Can follow simple instructions

Can throw and catch small and large balls

1 Give the children bean bags and ask them to practise throwing and catching them.

2 Some children will prefer to practise throwing and catching on their own.

Always have a high adult-to-child ratio during physical activities to help reduce the risk of accidents.

WHAT TO DO

- Follow steps one and two to encourage the children to practise throwing and catching.
- Tie the rope to two chairs and pull the rope taut.
- Ask for a volunteer to show how to throw a ball over and under the rope.
- Ask for two volunteers to try throwing and catching the ball over the rope.
- Lay out the remaining equipment and ask the children to practise throwing and catching in pairs and on their own.

10

I can slide

Materials and preparation

a selection of small equipment that the children can jump on and over · a large area of clear floor space

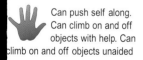
Can push self along. Can climb on and off objects with help. Can climb on and off objects unaided

Can remove and put on socks and shoes. Can dress and undress independently

Stop the children regularly to let a few of them show their ideas to the rest of the group.

1 Ask the children to lie on their fronts and then pull themselves along using just their arms and hands.

2 Ask the children to turn over and try pulling themselves along using their arms and hands and pushing themselves along using their legs and feet.

WHAT TO DO

- Ask the children to take off their shoes and socks and follow steps one and two.
- Spread out the apparatus and ask the children to try travelling on their fronts and backs over the apparatus.

TIPS This activity gives you lots of opportunities to assess each child's gross motor skills.
- Praise children constantly – it will encourage everyone to join in to their full ability.
- Join in on steps one and two so that the children can see exactly what you want them to do.

MY SENSES

This chapter focuses on the five senses. The activities give children many opportunities to respond imaginatively to sounds, sights, smells, tastes and touch, to use their senses, and to react in a creative, open way that develops their communication skills. Remember to allow for any hearing or sight difficulties the children may have. Doing the activities may also expose a child who has one of these difficulties. If this happens, alert your colleagues, and urge the parents to take the child to the doctor for a check up.

Activities in this chapter

1 What am I talking about?

 Can understand how prepositions are used to describe place

 Can concentrate for a reasonable length of time

▶ WHAT TO DO

- Choose an object somewhere in sight in the nursery.
- Describe where it is.
- Use model language such as big, small, in front of, behind, next to, near, rough, smooth, hard, soft.
- Ask the group to guess what you're talking about.
- Now ask one of the children to try.
- You can extend the activity further by asking one of the children to describe an object for everyone else to guess what they are talking about.

2 Seeing game

 Can walk, hop, and stand still

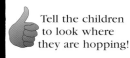 You will need lots of space, so this is a good game to play outside.

 Tell the children to look where they are hopping!

Play this game in the same way as the game Traffic Lights, but hold coloured objects in the air instead.

Game rules

- The red object means stand still.
- The yellow object means hop.
- The green object means skip.

Tell the group they are not allowed to use their voices. This will help keep the atmosphere calm.

3 Kim's game

Materials and preparation
- tray • sponge
- hairbrush • flannel • clementine
- jug • shampoo

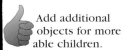 Recognises when something is the same or different

Can take turns. Can participate in group activities led by an adult

Add additional objects for more able children.

This verion of the traditional game is ideal for developing memory skills.

▶ WHAT TO DO

- Ask the children to look carefully at the objects on the table and to tell you what they are.
- Tell the children to close their eyes. Remove one of the objects.
- When the children open their eyes ask them what is missing.
- Make the game harder by removing more than one object at a time.

Feely bags

Materials and preparation

- 6 bags • 9 familiar objects
- place one object in three bags and two objects in three bags

To use language that describes shape, size and quantity

To touch a familiar object and express a reaction

To express the difference between hard and soft

Extend the activity by wrapping objects in paper. Ask the children to try to identify the objects by touch.

This can form a follow-up activity to What's inside the boxes? (8) page 34.

1 Ask the children to close their eyes and take turns to feel inside each bag. Ask the questions on the right.

2 Empty the bags and talk about what was inside them. Ask if the objects were big, small, hard or soft.

Questions

- Tell me about what you can feel. Does it feel hard or soft? (If children confuse these concepts, show them a hard object and a soft object for comparison.)
- How big is the object? (If the children pause for too long, show them some objects for comparison.)
- How many things can you feel? Are they the same?

Hot and cold

Materials and preparation

- bowl of ice • rubber gloves
- mittens • tissue paper
- bowl of warm water

To talk about their experiences to a small group

To express the concepts of cold and warm

Remove the ice from the freezer a few minutes before the activity to avoid freezer burn.

Warn the children never to put their hands anywhere near hot water. Explain that you are using only warm water for this activity.

Give the following instructions:

1 Show the children the ice cubes. Explain how they are made and that they are frozen water.

2 Let the children take turns to feel the ice cubes. Ask them to describe how the ice feels.

3 Ask the children to experiement holding the ice through the rubber gloves, mittens and tissues.

4 Introduce the bowl of warm water and repeat steps two and three with reference to the water.

Questions

Exploring the ice cubes
- How does it feel?
- What happens if you hold the ice for a long time?
- What does the ice feel like through the rubber gloves/mittens/tissues?
- What happens to the rubber gloves/mittens/tissues if you hold the ice on them for a long time?
- Which item protects your hands from the ice most?
- Which item keeps your hands dry?

Exploring the warm water
- How does it feel?
- What does the water feel like on bare hands?
- Does it feel different to the ice cubes? How?
- What does the water feel like through the rubber gloves/mittens/tissues?
- Which item protects your hands best/keeps your hands dry?

Dry and wet printing

Materials and preparation
• powder paint • newspaper
• chalk • sheets of A3 paper
• bowls of clean water

To control a paintbrush and chalk to make a mark

To express the concepts of wet and dry

To explore the properties of chalk and paint

When the handprints have dried, ask the children where they think the water has gone.

This is a creative activity allowing children to build on their experiences of wet and dry.

1 Ask the questions on the right, then let the children make handprints with the chalk and paint.

2 End the activity by washing hands. Talk about why and how we clean our hands.

Questions

- What happens to the powder paint when we add water to it? (Let the children mix the paints to see what happens.)
- Which is wet – the paint or the chalk?
- What do you think the chalk is made of? Is it watery or powdery?
- Why is the paint wet? What is it made of?
- After the children have made the handprints ask which ones are wet. (If the children find this difficult to answer remind them of how they made the paint.)

I can touch with my hands ...

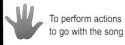
To perform actions to go with the song

Is confident in a familiar environment

To make up their own words about the senses through song

This is a song you can sing as a follow-up to any of the activities in this chapter.

▶ **WHAT TO DO**

- Teach the children the tune to the song.
- Follow steps one to five for the words and actions.
- Ask the children to make up their own words and actions for other verses.

I can touch with my hands, oh! yes I

can.   I can touch   with my   hands,

oh!   yes   I   can.

1 I can touch with my hands, oh! yes I can.

2 I can see with my eyes, oh! yes I can.

3 I can hear with my ears, oh! yes I can.

4 I can smell with my nose, oh! yes I can.

5 I can taste with my tongue, oh! yes I can.

What's inside the boxes?

Materials and preparation

- a selection of familiar objects • four boxes • Place one object in two boxes and two objects in two boxes

To explore sound using different materials

a b

To listen attentively and talk about their experience

Shake each box in turn and tell the children they are going to use their ears to identify objects.

1 Show the children one box at a time. Ask them to shake the box and guess what is inside. Scribe their responses.

2 When everyone has guessed what is inside each box, open the boxes. Talk about each object and the sound it makes.

3 Refill the boxes with objects the children have chosen. Ask them to identify the objects by sound.

Questions

- What sound can you hear from the first box?
- Can you hear something rolling or sliding in the box?
- Do you think it has flat sides or round sides? Why?
- Can you hear lots of things or just one?
- Tell me more about the sounds you can hear from the box.
- What do you think is inside the box?

Tell the children their sound descriptions are more important than guessing the object correctly.

Loud and quiet sounds

Materials and preparation

- a selection of musical instruments – some that make loud sounds and some that make quiet sounds

To experiment with a variety of musical instruments

To experiment to find out how things work

This is a noisy activity, so it is best done in small groups to contain the noise.

1 Show the children how to make loud sounds with some of the instruments. Ask the children to experiment making loud sounds.

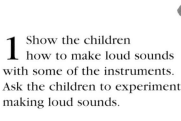

2 Repeat step one but make quiet sounds and ask the children to do the same. Ask which instruments are best for making loud or quiet sounds.

Questions

- Can someone choose an instrument and show me how to play it?
- Can anyone think of another way to play the instrument?
- Which instrument do you think will make the loudest noise?
- What do the loud noises sound like?
- How can you make a quiet sound?
- What do the quiet noises sound like?

Shake, scrape or hit?

Materials and preparation

- a variety of instruments that the children can shake, scrap and hit

To show interest in other children. Can take turns

To sort a variety of objects

To shake, hit, and scrape an instrument to produce sound

Sit on the floor around the instruments to make this a really experimental activity for the children.

▶ WHAT TO DO

- Ask one child to pick an instrument and show the group how it might be played. Repeat with all the instruments.
- Talk about the sounds the instruments make.
- Show the children the connection between the sounds the instruments make and how they are played – by shaking, scraping or hitting.
- Ask the children to sort the instruments according to how they are played.

11

Listening inside and outside

Materials and preparation

- cassette tape recorder • cassette tape with everyday sounds • laminated pictures of the sounds on the cassette tape • two hoops

To use language to describe inside and outside. To sort everyday sounds

To talk about events in their own life. To talk about where they have heard familiar sounds before

You could introduce any combination of sounds for this activity.

1 Let the children take it in turns operating the cassette tape recorder. Make sure they know how to use the start, stop and pause buttons.

▶ WHAT TO DO

- Show the children how to use the cassette tape recorder.
- Explain that each sound on the cassette tape has a matching picture card.
- Leave the children to work in pairs matching the sounds to the picture cards.
- Leave the materials out so that the children can return to the activity during free-play times.

EXTENSION IDEAS

- Make a cassette tape and laminated cards of day time and night time sounds. Ask the children to identify the sounds and group them accordingly.
- Photograph the musical instruments used in Shake, scrape, or hit? (10) and record the sounds they make. Do the activity with these sounds.

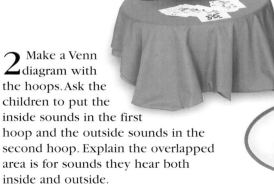

2 Make a Venn diagram with the hoops. Ask the children to put the inside sounds in the first hoop and the outside sounds in the second hoop. Explain the overlapped area is for sounds they hear both inside and outside.

Everyday smells

Materials and preparation

• fragrant flower • coffee beans • fresh bread • lemon • orange • tea bags • ginger • parmesan cheese • perfumed soap • fresh herbs • notebook • pen

 To talk about and react to smells

 To participate in a group activity led by an adult

This activity is guaranteed to be a talking point for days afterwards!

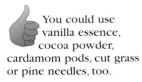 You could use vanilla essence, cocoa powder, cardamom pods, cut grass or pine needles, too.

▶ WHAT TO DO

• Ask the children to smell each object and describe the smell.
• Scribe the children's responses.
• If the children find it hard to find descriptive words, help them by introducing words such as sweet, perfumed, sour and so on.
• Then ask the children to close their eyes and try to identify each object in turn by smell alone.

Use objects that the children can pick up and hold to their noses easily.

Describing smells

Materials and preparation

• fragrant flower • coffee beans • fresh bread • lemon • orange • tea bags • ginger • parmesan cheese • perfumed soap • fresh herbs • notebook • pen

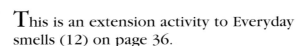 To describe and react to smells

To participate in a group activity led by an adult

This is an extension activity to Everyday smells (12) on page 36.

 Talk about warning smells, such as when food has gone bad.

 Extend the activity by introducing more smells for the children to describe.

▶ WHAT TO DO

• Talk about the descriptive words the children used to describe each object in Everyday smells (12).
• Ask one child to choose one object and describe its smell to the rest of the group. Encourage the child to use the same descriptive language you scribed in Everyday smells (12).
  The child who guesses the object correctly then has a turn describing an object to the class.

Fizzy tasting

Materials and preparation

• one bottle of sparkling water • one bottle of still water • plastic cups

 To talk about their own observations

 To follow simple instructions and take turns

 Make sure the cups you use are clean.

Allow older children to open the bottles themselves under supervision.

▶ WHAT TO DO

- Ask the children if they have tasted sparkling water before and what it tastes like.
- Open the bottle of sparkling water. Ask the children to describe the noise as you open the bottle.
- Pour water into the cups – one for each child.
- Ask the children to taste and describe the water.
- Repeat with the still water.
- Ask the children to tell you the difference between the two kinds of water.

15

Sweet and sour

Materials and preparation

• sugar • lemon juice • apple juice • orange juice • still water • cups • notebook • pen • pastels • felt-tipped pens • paint • pencils • paper

 To talk about their own observations

To talk about and react to different tastes

Extend the activity by asking the children to identify the drinks by taste alone.

This is an extension to Fizzy tasting (14) page 37 for older or more-able children.

▶ WHAT TO DO

- Pour each kind of drink into cups – one for each child.
- Ask the children to describe each taste in turn. Scribe their comments.
- Introduce descriptive words such as sweet, sour, bitter and sugary.
- Pour another set of drinks for each child but add lemon juice to these drinks. Ask the children to describe the new flavours.
- Repeat the step above but add sugar instead of lemon juice.
- Ask the children to draw pictures to show how they feel about each taste.

MY FEELINGS

F eeling special, frightened, brave, happy, sad, cross, excited, angry,
imaginative and glad are all emotions experienced by children. It is
important to recognise each emotion and not just focus on 'positive' emotions
such as happy and glad. The activities in this chapter encourage children to
explore their emotions through group discussion, role play, creative activities
and by using stories as a starting point. It is vital that you listen to and value
each child's contribution so that he or she will feel safe and special in the nursery.

Activities in this chapter

1

Good days, sad days

Exploring things that make a good day
or a sad day and how we feel if we
make someone else happy or sad

2

Happy times

Based on the popular rhyme "Girls and boys
come out to play", this activity lets children explore
what affects their feelings and moods

3

Feeling special

A discussion activity using props to talk about
occasions that have made children feel special and why

4

Thank you for my friends

A fun song for children to learn to help them
understand why having friends makes them feel good
and why they should be kind to their friends

5

I hear thunder

Using a popular nursery rhyme to explore how
the weather affects children's feelings

6

Little Miss Muffet

Using another popular nursery rhyme to talk
about why children are often scared of minibeasts
with tips on how to reassure children about
things that frighten them

7

Feeling brave

Based on a popular story, this activity gives children
plenty of opportunities to explore how they feel
when they are brave and has a fun step-by-step
snake-making activity

8

When I'm angry

Based on a popular novel, this activity helps
children talk about what makes them feel angry and
how they can control their feelings

9

People we love

Using photographs of family and friends to encourage
children to think about why these people are
special, and drawing pictures of them

10

My pets

Learning a fun nursery rhyme that encourages
children to think about how they feel about the pets
their family, relatives or friends may have

11

Animal feelings

An extension to activity 10, to encourage
children to think about the feelings of animals and
how they can recognise them

12

Puzzle pictures

Making puzzles with facial expressions that show
typical feelings. The children match the puzzle
pieces to make the correct expressions

13

Making masks

A fun mask-making activity that reinforces
all the activities in this chapter, using templates
provided in the resources section

14

Theatrical masks

Opportunities to explore theatrical masks and how
feelings can be emphasised in pictures. Step-by-step
instructions on how to make comedy and tragedy masks

1   Good days, sad days

 To talk about events in own life

 To participate in a group activity led by an adult

 To participate in a question and answer session

TIPS   You could simplify this chart for younger children by using symbols as well as words.
- Ask the children to think of something they can do to ensure their friends have a good day. Write an action plan and make sure the children carry out their suggestions.

▶ WHAT TO DO

- Tell the children you have had a good day because you received a special invitation.
- Ask if they can think of one good thing that has happened to them today.
- Scribe the children's responses on a chart.
- Tell the children about something that made you sad, for example forgetting to bring in a book you had promised to lend someone.
- Ask the children to tell you about something that made them feel sad and scribe their responses.

2   Happy times

 Enjoys singing and joins in with others

 To participate in a group activity led by an adult

 To listen and respond to a rhyme

Extend this activity by singing the popular song 'If you're happy and you know it'.

Girls and boys come out to play

Girls and boys come out to play,

The moon is shining bright as day.

Leave your supper and leave your sleep,

And come with your playfellows

into the street.

Come with a whoop, and come

with a call,

Come with a good will, or come

not at all.

Come let us dance on the open green,

And she who holds longest

shall be our queen.

▶ WHAT TO DO

- Teach the children the nursery rhyme
- Ask them to sing the rhyme holding hands, skipping in a large circle.
- Talk about the feelings in the song and ask the children if they think it is a happy song or a sad song. Be prepared for a variety of responses!

TIP   Some children find it hard to learn things by heart. Teach them the rhyme as follows:
- Explain what the rhyme is about and point out any difficult words.
- Say two lines at a time and ask the children to repeat the lines.
- Say the whole rhyme together.
- Repeat the rhyme often with the children.

3   Feeling special

Materials and prepartion

A4 size homemade book, with a photograph of the nursery children on the front.

 Enjoys looking at books

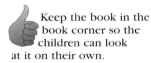 Talks about important events in own life

Keep the book in the book corner so the children can look at it on their own.

Extend the activity by asking the children to bring in something that is special to them and ask them to talk about it to the rest of the group.

Carry out this activity over several weeks so that each child has the opportunity to talk about what makes him or her feel special.

I was a Bridesmaid

my Birthday

Bring out the book regularly for the children to look at and read.

▶ WHAT TO DO

- Ask the children to bring in photographs of special occasions, such as weddings, parties, and holidays, which you can stick into the book.
- Ask one of the children to pick one of the photographs to talk about. Stick the photograph in the homemade book and scribe the child's comments.
- Repeat this activity over several days until all the children have chosen a photograph to describe and put in the book.

4   Thank you for my friends

 Enjoys singing and joins in with others

Extend the activity by asking the children what they can do to make their friends feel special.

This is a good follow-on activity to Feeling special (3) page 40. Explain that having good friends makes you feel good and that it is important to treat them well.

▶ WHAT TO DO

- Teach the children the song and make up actions to go with the words.

When we're play_ing in the park, Thank you for my friends. When it's cold and wet and dark, Thank you for my friends. When we're go _ ing to the fair, When we all have sweets to share, Ev_en when they're cross and they pull my hair, Thank you for my friends.

5   I hear thunder

 Can talk about own experiences

 Enjoys singing and joining in with others

Songs and rhymes are ideal for starting points for talking about different kinds of weather.

I   hear   thun _ der,   I   hear   thun _ der,

Hark   don't   you?   Hark   don't   you?

Pit_ter pat_ter rain drops, Pit_ter pat_ter rain drops.

I'm   wet   through,   So   are   you.

EXTENSION IDEAS

- Ask the children to act out the rhyme.
- Tell the children to clap their hands for gentle rain and to stamp their feet for heavy rain. Use musical instruments to make the thunder and long ribbons to represent the lightening.

▶ WHAT TO DO

- Teach the children the rhyme and repeat it as a group.
- Ask the children if they are scared of thunder and why.
- Ask if other kinds of weather scare them.
- Ask if any of the children like thunder. Ask how it makes them feel.
- Talk about sunshine and ask the children how they feel on bright sunny days.

---

6   Little Miss Muffet

Materials and prepartion

Selection of pictures ready to look at including spiders, night time, tigers, and other scary things

 To listen and respond to a rhyme

 To share own experiences with others

 Make a spider out of card and act out the rhyme with the children.

Recite the rhyme Little Miss Muffet and then talk to the children about what frightens them and why.

Little Miss Muffet

Little Miss Muffet
sat on her tuffet
eating her curds and whey.
Along came a spider and
sat down beside her
and frightened
Miss Muffet away.

EXTENSION IDEAS

- Read the story 'Can't you sleep little bear' by M. Waddell and B. Firth, Walker Books. Talk about why the bear was frightened and what frightens the children.
- Ask the children who they turn to when they are frightened and how that person helps them.

TIP Reassure children that it is natural to feel frightened about some things and that they can come to you or other responsible adults if they need to.

Feeling brave

Materials and prepartion

- selection of junk · paper
material · card · Playdough · pipe
cleaners · polystyrene balls
· sticky tape · glue paint · scissors
· wool (variety of colours)

Enjoys listening to stories. Explores junk and paint

Can use sticky tape, glue, scissors. Can use junk objects to create a model

Encourage the children to use all the materials when they make their own snakes.

This activity is based on the story 'Do You Dare' by Paul and Emma Rogers, Orchard Books 1991.

1 Read the story. Ask the children to think of things that did not scare them in the story. Show them the materials and say you are going to make a snake from the junk.

EXTENSION IDEAS

- Ask the children to make the following scary objects:
the witch's hat
the witch's broomstick
the spider

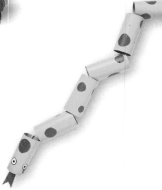

2 Paint the toilet rolls yellow. Add red dots when the paint is dry.

3 Join the toilet rolls together with a long piece of string.

4 Add a card tongue and eyes. Ask the children to make their own snakes.

When I'm angry

Enjoys listening to stories

Talks freely with other children and familar adults

This activity can be done in the last 15 minutes of a session, once a week during this topic. The children soon get used to listening to and responding to stories about feelings.

Introduce the concept of feeling angry by reading 'I feel Angry' by Brian Moses and Mike Gordon, Wayland Publishers 1991 and ask the questions on the right.

Questions

- Have you ever felt angry?
- When? What happened?
- What did you do?
- Did you look like the little boy in the story?
- Why do you think he felt like a balloon about to burst? Have you ever felt like that?
- Why do you think the boy in the story threw his toys around? Do you think that made him feel better or worse? What do you think his mum or dad said when they saw his toys thrown around?
- Has your friend ever been really angry with you?
- How did you feel? Were you scared? Worried? Or didn't you mind?

People we love

Materials and preparation

A3 and A4 paper (a variety of colours) · pencils · glue · glue sticks · powder paint mixed and ready to use (a variety of colours) · paint brushes · tissue paper (cut up ready for the children to use for collage) · chalk · crayons · charcoal

Explores properties of paint, chalk, crayon, charcoal, and collage

Can talk freely

Shows interest in other children and familiar adults. Can share own experiences with others

Ask more able children to write something for the person to go with the picture.

Talk about people we love and ask the children to make pictures of someone they love.

Sebastian's picture of his friend Jenny.

Julianne's picture of her friend Martha.

Hannah's picture of her Auntie.

Questions

- What can you see on the table?
- How can we use these things to make a picture?
- Can you think of someone you would like to make a picture for?
- Who?
- Can you think of someone who makes you laugh / you like to play with / is kind to you / lives in your house / lives far away?
- Tell me about that person.
- Can you make a picture to give to one of these people?
- What could you use to make your picture? Let the children choose and use any of the materials you have put out.

My pets

Materials and preparation

· pictures of typical family pets

Listens and responds to rhymes

Allows other children to take turns in conversation. Listens when others are speaking. Speaks clearly

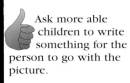

You can extend this activity by talking about the children's feelings towards other animals, too.

I love little pussy

I love little pussy, her coat
is so warm,

And if I don't hurt her she'll
do me no harm.

So I'll not pull her tail, nor
drive her away,

But pussy and I very
gently will play.

▶ WHAT TO DO

- Read the poem to the children while stroking an imaginary cat.
- Ask the children if they have a pet or know anyone who has a pet.
- Ask them to talk about their feelings towards the pet.
- If any of the children are scared of a pet, give them time to talk about their feelings.
- Ask how they can treat their pets nicely.

Animal feelings

Materials and preparation

Pictures of animals displaying different emotions, including purring cats, scared cats, sleepy dogs, energetic dogs and wild animals

EXTENSION IDEAS

- Set up a vet's corner and let the children role play caring for animals.
- Ask the children to paint pictures of animals expressing different feelings.
- Make a wall display with the animal pictures and scribe the children's comments about animals and their feelings.

This can form a follow up activity to My pets (10) page 43.

To talk freely with other children and familiar adults

To show an interest in the experiences of others

▶ WHAT TO DO

- Show the children the pictures and ask how they think the animals feel.
- Discuss the importance of understanding animals' feelings and what will upset animals.
- Let the children think about what makes their family pets happy and sad and what the children can do to treat their pets well.
- Get leaflets from the RSPCA and Blue Cross and talk about what these organisations do.

Puzzle pictures

Materials and preparation

thin card · scissors · colouring pencils · sticky-backed plastic

Can complete simple fit-together jigsaws

Can play purposefully on own

You could make the puzzles with the templates provided or ask the children to draw their own faces.

These templates appear on pages 62–63.

You could make the puzzles with the pictures used in Animal feelings (11) page 44.

1 Enlarge the templates on a photocopier or piece of graph paper. Cut out the templates and trace around them on to a piece of thin card.

2 Paint the picture or ask the children to paint it. Cover the picture in sticky-backed plastic to strengthen it.

3 Cut each puzzle face into pieces – two for younger children and four for older children. Leave the puzzle pieces out for the children to do.

Making masks

Materials and preparation
· thin card · powder paints
· hole puncher · hole reinforcers

To control a
paintbrush
to make a mark

To follow
simple
instructions

To play
imaginatively as
part of a group

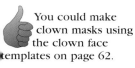
You could make
clown masks using
the clown face
templates on page 62.

This activity is perfect for reinforcing all the
work done on feelings in this chapter.

1 Enlarge the face
templates in Puzzle
pictures (12). Trace around
the templates on to the
thin card. Cut out holes
for the eyes and the string.

2 Ask the children to
choose one of the facial
expressions to paint. Leave
the masks to dry. Knot a
piece of string at each of
the holes and tie the masks
around the children's heads.

3 Ask the children to
make up and act out
stories relevant to the
expressions on their masks.

Theatrical masks

Materials and preparation
· selection of pictures
of theatrical masks · newspaper
· balloons · PVA glue · powder paints
· material to decorate masks

Can follow simple
instructions

To play imaginatively
as part of a group

Make up a story with
the children using
the masks. Invite
parents and relatives in to
watch the performance.

Warn the children
before you pop the
balloons so that they
are not frightened.

Show the children the pictures of the theatrical
masks. Talk about the exaggerated expressions and
then help the children make their own masks.

1 Blow up a balloon for
each child. Dip newspaper
into the PVA glue. Lay the
newspaper over one
half of the balloon.

2 Build up several layers
of newspaper. Allow the
paper to dry out in between
layers. Leave to dry overnight.

3 Carefully pop the
balloon with a pin.
Draw exaggerated features
on the masks and cut out
the eyes and mouth.

4 Paint a base colour
on the mask and then
let the children add their
own individual features
to their masks.

5 Use the masks for
role play activities and
encourage the children to
make up their own happy
and sad stories.

LOOKING AFTER MYSELF

The activities in this chapter encourage children to develop personal responsibility and independence by learning how to look after themselves. Children are given opportunities to develop an understanding of the importance of personal hygiene. They are encouraged to think about how to keep themselves healthy and strong as well as how to protect themselves at home and outside. The important issue of road safety is covered as well as safety in the home and there are many role play and dressing-up activities to reinforce the information learnt.

Activities in this chapter

1
Keeping myself clean
Discussing the importance of personal hygiene and how to keep clean

2
Washing my clothes
Looking at why we need to clean our clothes and experimenting with different solutions to find the best way of doing this

3
Looking after my teeth
An extension to Keeping myself clean (1) that focuses on oral hygiene and which foods are good or bad for your teeth

4
Am I healthy?
A discussion activity that encourages children to think about which foods are full of nutritional value and which aren't

5
Sleepy head
Using a popular nursery rhyme as a starting point for discussing the importance of sleep and what happens if you don't sleep enough

6
Safety in the home
Using the home corner as a focal point to talk about how and why accidents occur at home, how to avoid them and what to do if an accident does happen

7
Safety in the street
A role play activity that reinforces road safety and teaches the Green Cross Code

8
Keeping dry in the rain
A fun activity experimenting with the waterproof properties of various materials to show children how to protect themselves from wet weather

9
Protective clothes
Learning about the clothes people wear in extreme climates and choosing the best clothing for different weather conditions

10
The correct shoes
Examining the properties of different kinds of footwear and deciding which footwear is appropriate for specific kinds of weather

Keeping myself clean

Materials and preparation

· soap · flannel · sponge · bubble bath ·
shampoo · bowls of water · towels ·
toothbrush · toothpaste

Can talk about
own experiences

Knows the difference
between clean and dirty

Understands the need to
keep themselves clean

EXTENSION IDEAS

· To extend this activity for
older children, ask them
to write a list, or to draw
pictures to explain all the
different things they do
to keep themselves clean.

▶ WHAT TO DO

· Talk about the objects on
the table. Show the group
the soap.

· Ask them why we use
soap to wash ourselves
and why not just water?

· Ask one child to show
the group how to wash
his or her hands and face.

· Ask the children to tell
you what would happen
if they didn't wash.

· Ask them to tell you
about how they brush
their teeth, have a bath,
and how they use the
resources on the table
to help keep
themselves clean.

· Put some chocolate or
tomato sauce on a doll's
face and ask the children
how they would clean
it off.

Washing my clothes

T̲alk about how clothes get dirty and why
you need to wash them, then introduce the
children to the materials on the table.

Materials and preparation

· 4 bowls of warm water · scrubbing
brushes · a range of clothes with stains
on them – for example tomato sauce,
baked beans, coffee, coca cola · washing
powder · washing liquids
· clothes line · clothes pegs

Knowing the difference
between clean and dirty

Understands the
need to clean
their clothes

TIP Make sure you have
space for the material
to be hung up to dry –
on a radiator, or a
washing line inside
or outside.

· Ensure you tell the
children they need to
use only a little washing
powder or liquid.

▶ WHAT TO DO

· Ask the children to look
closely at the material,
and to tell you what they
think made it dirty.

· Ask them to choose one
piece of material and to
wash it in their bowl of
water, using the washing
powder or liquid.

· Ask the group to wash
their material to make it
as clean as they can.

· As they are washing
ask 'Why is your water
changing colour? Is the
dirty stain going away?
Where is the best place
to put your material
to dry?'

· End the activity by asking
the children to hang the
clothes to dry. Show
them how to use the
clothes pegs.

3

Looking after my teeth

Materials and preparation

new toothbrush for each child · toothpaste · apples

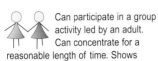

Can participate in a group activity led by an adult. Can concentrate for a reasonable length of time. Shows confidence in a new situation

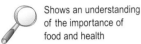

Shows an understanding of the importance of food and health

Reinforce the visit by talking about it regularly and asking the children how they look after their teeth.

Invite a health visitor, school nurse, dentist, or dental nurse into the nursery to talk about oral hygiene for this activity.

▶ WHAT TO DO

- Ask the visitor to talk to the children about brushing their teeth, and eating healthy foods. Ask the visitor to bring a model of a set of teeth, a giant toothbrush and examples of healthy food so that the experience is visual for the children, too.
- Ask the visitor to show the children how to brush their teeth correctly and ensure each child is given time to practise brushing his or her teeth.

4

Am I healthy?

Materials and preparation

· a selection of foods – some healthy and some unhealthy

Shows an understanding of the importance of food and health

This is an extension activity to Looking after my teeth (3) page 48.

▶ WHAT TO DO

- Ask the children to tell you what the health visitor said about healthy foods.
- Show the children a variety of foods and ask which foods are healthy/ unhealthy?
- Talk about foods that are bad for their teeth such as sugary sweets.

Apple

Sweets

Orange

Pepper

Bread

Lettuce

Carrots

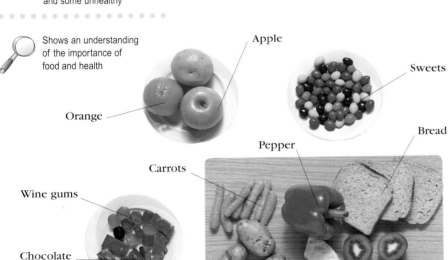

Carrots

Wine gums

Chocolate

Ginger

Potatoes

Tomatoes

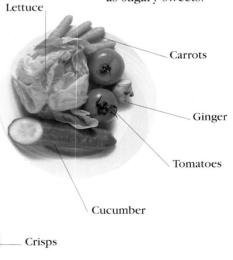

Cucumber

Nuts and raisins

Crisps

Jelly beans

5 Sleepy head

 Can participate in group activities led by an adult

 Listens and responds to rhymes

TIP Some children find it quite hard to learn things by heart. Teach them the rhymes as follows:
- Explain what the rhyme is about.
- Point out any difficult words.
- Say two lines at a time and ask the children to repeat the lines.
- Say the whole rhyme together.
- Repeat the rhyme at regular intervals with the children.

Use these rhymes to help children understand the importance of sleep.

Go to bed late
Go to bed late,
Stay very small,
Go to bed early,
Grow very tall

Down with the lambs
Down with the lambs,
Up with the lark,
Run to bed, children,
Before it gets dark

▶ WHAT TO DO

- Talk about the importance of going to bed early and how the children would feel if they went to bed late every night. Ask: How would you feel if you went to bed late? How would you feel the next morning? Would you feel wide awake?
- Discuss occasions when it is difficult to sleep – when excited, anxious, poorly, if there is too much noise.
- Talk about people who have to work at night and how they sleep during the day.
- Discuss bedtime routines and how they differ in different families.

6 Safety in the home

 Shows an understanding of health and related issues

Can use events in own life as a starting point for imaginative play

EXTENSION IDEAS
- Set up a doctor's surgery and encourage the children to role play a doctor treating a patient. Provide lots of bandages so that the children can learn how to tie slings. Make signs to go in the surgery and waiting room and provide paper for writing patient notes.
- Invite a nurse to come in and talk to the children about basic first aid.

Use the home corner as a starting point to talk about the important issue of safety in the home.

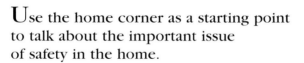 Use toy irons and kettles to stress the importance of not touching hot objects and putting things in sockets and so on.

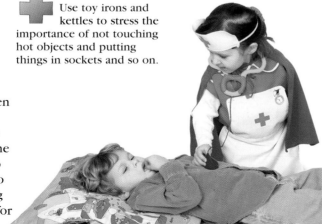

▶ WHAT TO DO

- Ask the children to tell you about any accidents that have happened in their home.
- Get leaflets from Royal Society for the Prevention of Accidents (RoSPA) and talk about safety in the home.
- Teach the children about the emergency services and when they should dial 999.

7 Safety in the street

This activity gives the children the opportunity to reinforce their learning through role play.

Materials and preparation
· zebra crossing · 'lollipop' stick

 Can purposefully with other children

 Can use events in own life as a starting point for imaginative play

Invite a 'lollipop' person, or police officer into the nursery to talk about safety outside.

Make a zebra crossing by painting four pieces of A3 paper black. Stick alternate pieces to pieces of white A3 paper.

▶ WHAT TO DO

· Talk about why the children must hold an adult's hand when walking on a pavement near a road.
· Explain the Green Cross Code to them and why it is important always to follow its rules.

GREEN CROSS CODE

· Use a pelican or zebra crossing if you see one. Otherwise, find a safe place to cross, away from parked cars.
· Hold an adult's hand. Look right, then left, then right again.
· When the road is clear, start to cross looking both ways as you walk.

---

8 Keeping dry in the rain

This activity is ideal for a wet day when children can test out the waterproof properties of different clothes.

Materials and preparation
· wet weather clothes ·
dry, warm weather clothes

 Can talk about own experience of weather

 Exploring the difference between wet and dry

EXTENSION IDEAS

· Introduce a weather chart and symbols. Discuss the kind of weather each symbol represents. At the start of each session introduce the weather chart and symbols. Ask the children to describe what the weather is like and pick the appropriate symbol or symbols to put on the chart.

▶ WHAT TO DO

· Talk about the clothes on the table.
· Ask the group to choose the clothes which would protect them from the rain.
· Talk about how the rain clothes are different to the hot weather clothes.
· If it's raining, ask the group to put on their coats, hats and wellington boots so that you can go outside for a few minutes.
· When you come back inside talk about how the clothes protected them.

Protective clothes

· pictures of people who live in extreme climates such as the desert and the North Pole · a variety of clothing for different environments

Responds to pictures of other people in other places

Shows confidence in a new situation

Listens when others are speaking

EXTENSION IDEAS

Invite some firefighters into the nursery to show the children how their uniforms and equipment protect them when fighting fires.

Children love to dress up. This activity encourages children to learn while dressing up.

▶ WHAT TO DO

· Show the children the photographs and talk about what the people are wearing and how their clothes are suitable for their environments.
· Lay out the clothes and talk about the environments the clothes are suitable for.
· Pick an environment for each child and ask them to choose the correct clothes to dress up in.

Questions

· Can you describe the clothes/hats/shoes the people are wearing in the pictures?
· What sort of hat would you wear in hot/wet/cold weather? Why?
· Why do you need sunblock on hot sunny days?

10

The correct shoes

· a variety of shoes for different kinds of weather that have buckles, laces, Velcro, rough and smooth soles

Can remove/put on shoes.

Can sort objects

Understands the concepts of wet and dry, warm and cold, rough and smooth

Can talk about their own experiences of the weather

You can make this activity as simple or complicated as you like by having more or fewer shoes.

▶ WHAT TO DO

· Lay the shoes out and ask the children which shoes have laces / Velcro? How many are there? How many plimsolls can you see?
· Ask them to look at the underneath of the shoes and to tell you which ones are rough and which ones are smooth.
· Pick a party shoe or sandle and ask 'would this shoe protect your foot from the rain? Do you think it would keep your foot warm?'
· Ask questions about the other shoes, too.
· Let the children practice tying laces, buckling shoes and so on.

MY FAVOURITE THINGS

The activities in this chapter allow children the opportunity to talk about and reflect upon their likes and dislikes. They help children to differentiate their feelings and understand the concept of liking one thing more than another. Many of the activities also promote mathematics by focusing on colour and shape. Colour concepts are also developed through creative activities and many language and literacy activities help children learn to recognise and name colours. The activities will provide children with many opportunities to talk, share ideas and feel special.

Activities in this chapter

1   My favourite colour

Materials and preparation

* crepe paper • tissue paper
* sticky paper • tawky paper
* shiny paper wool • glue • glue sticks
* scissors • A3 sugar paper

Place all the materials on a covered table

Can name and recognise colours

Explores properties of material to make a collage

Can use scissors appropriately

EXTENSION IDEAS

* Ask the children to make a collage using their favourite materials.
* For older children, make a bar chart showing how many children like which colour best.

▶ WHAT TO DO

* Show the children the collage materials and ask them to sort them according to colour.
* Ask the children to name the colours and to describe them.
* Let the children pick their favourite colours to make a collage.

Questions

* How will you make the material stay on your piece of paper?
* What will your collage picture look like?
* Will you stick the materials next to each other or on top of each other?
* Will you make a collage picture of something or will you stick the material anywhere?

---

2   Fruit and vegetable printing

Materials and preparation

Fruit and vegetables that are in season • powder paints • A3 sugar paper

Place the materials on a covered table

Can name and recognise colours

Explores paint

Questions

* Have you eaten any of the fruit or vegetables before?
* What did it/they taste like?
* Which is your favourite/least favourite fruit/vegetable?
* Describe the fruit/vegetables. What colour are they? What do they feel like?

Use this activity to reinforce the healthy eating concepts covered in *Am I healthy?* (4) page 48.

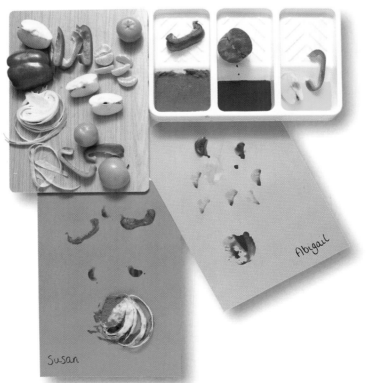

▶ WHAT TO DO

* Show the children the materials and ask the questions below.
* Let the children choose which materials they want to use to make prints.
* Ask the children to make the prints next to each other so that they can compare the shapes and colours.

You could extend the activity by asking the children to sort the food into fruit and vegetables.

3   My favourite shape

You can make this activity as simple or complex as you like by using more or fewer shapes.

Can name and recognise circles, squares, rectangles and triangles

Can join in with question and answer sessions

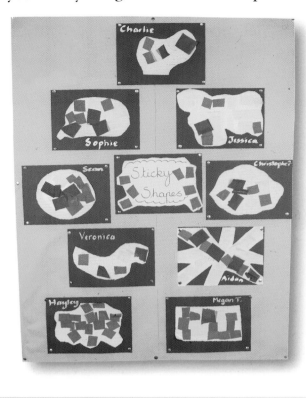

Extend the activity by introducing Plasticine. Ask the children to make their favourite 3-D shapes.

▶ WHAT TO DO

- Ask the children to look at the pictures you have drawn. Ask the questions below.
- Ask the children to pick their favourite shapes and make a collage with them.

Questions

- Can you describe the pictures?
- Can you see a circle/rectangle/square in one of the pictures?
- Which is your favourite shape?
- Can you show me a picture with your favourite shape in it?
- Can you draw your favourite shape?
- Can you colour the shape in your favourite colour?

---

4   My favourite weather

Enjoys singing and joins in with others

Talks about the weather

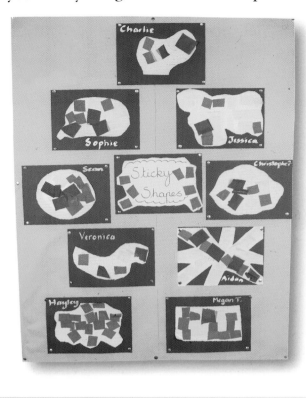

1. I love the sun, It shines on__ me,

God made the sun, And God made me.

▶ WHAT TO DO

- Teach the children the tune to the song.
- Follow steps one to five for the words.

This activity could be used as a follow-on from Keeping dry in the rain (8) page 50.

1 I love the sun,
It shines on me,
God made the sun,
And God made me.

2 I love the rain,
It splashes on me,
God made the rain,
And God made me.

3 I love the wind,
It blows around me,
God made the wind,
And God made me.

4 I love the snow,
It falls on me,
God made the snow,
And God made me.

5 I love the thunder,
It rumbles round me,
God made the thunder,
And God made me.

Ask the children to make up additional verses.

5 My favourite clothes

Materials and preparation

- the children's favourite clothes
- washing line · clothes pegs

Can recognise colours

Can participate in group activities led by an adult

Can take turns. Can speak clearly. Can join in with question and answer sessions

You will need each child's favourite item of clothing for this activity. Ask the parents to ensure the children all remember to bring clothes in!

You could extend this activity by asking children to talk about their favourite nursery toy for one minute.

▶ WHAT TO DO

- When the children come into the nursery, hang up their favourite clothes on the washing line.
- Talk about the clothes. Ask the children what they can see on the washing line, how many tops, trousers, socks and so on there are.
- Invite each child to come to the front of the class and speak for about their favourite item of clothing.
- If the children cannot think of anything to say, prompt them with questions: why is this your favourite item of clothing? Is it your favourite colour? Where did you buy it? Who bought it for you?

---

6 My favourite food

Materials and preparation

- packaging of the children's favourite foods · bread · shaped pastry cutters · butter or margarine · sandwich fillings

Can participate in group activities led by an adult

Can talk about and react to how different foods smell and taste

Shows an understanding of the importance of hygiene when handling food

Ask the children to bring in packaging from their favourite foods for this activity.

1 Show the children the sandwich ingredients. Let them butter the bread and choose their favourite-shaped pastry cutters.

2 Let the children choose their favourite sandwich filling and put it on one slice of bread. Show the children how to place the second slice directly over the first slice and cut out shapes with the pastry cutters.

Make sure the packaging the children bring into the nursery has been washed where necessary.

▶ WHAT TO DO

- Talk about the packaging the children have brought in. Ask them to tell you about their favourite food – what does it look like? do you eat it hot or cold? What does it taste like? How often do you eat it? Do you eat it straight from the package or do you cook it first? How do you cook it?

Introduce the group to the sandwich ingredients and tell them they are going to make their favourite sandwiches. Follow steps one and two to make the sandwiches.

Extend making a graph showing how many children like each filling best.

Materials and preparation

• salt • flour • mixing bowl • clay
• rolling pin • animal-shaped cutters
• Plasticine • model animals

 Can use a rolling pin and cutter appropriately

 Explores the properties of clay

 Use food colouring to colour the salt dough.

TIPS FOR USING CLAY

• Work each ball of clay in your hands just before you start the activity. This will make it more pliable for the children.
• Ask the group to try to bend, then push and pull the clay.
• Introduce clay tools and ask the children to experiment making marks in the clay.

If you do not have any clay, follow steps one and two below to make salt dough.

1 Add 1 part salt to 2 parts flour. Gradually add 1 part water to make a smooth firm consistency.

2 Knead the dough for 10 minutes. Leave to rest in an airtight container for 30 minutes before use.

3 Let the children roll out the salt dough (or clay) and use the cutters to create animal shapes.

4 Give the children broken-up sweets to decorate the animals. Bake in a cool oven until completely hardened.

Ask each child to pick their favourite model and make a table display with the children's models and the plastic models they used for reference.

▶ WHAT TO DO

• Show the children the clay or salt dough, rolling pin and cutters. Explain that they are going to make animal shapes with the cutters.
• Let the children roll out the clay or dough and choose their favourite animal-shaped cutters.
• Talk about each animal and ask the children why a particular animal is their favourite.
• Introduce the plasticine and model animals.
• Ask the children to make models of their favourite animals. They can use the model animals as reference if they want.

Colourful Plasticine will attract the children's interest more than dull colours.

My favourite toy

 Can talk freely with other children and familiar adults

 Explores materials

Can talk about experience of toys at home and at nursery

Ask each child to bring in their favourite toy from home for this activity.

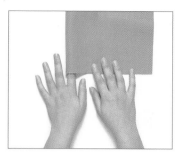

1 Show the children the materials and ask them to pick out their favourite coloured felt.

2 Fold over one edge of the felt twice the width of one finger.

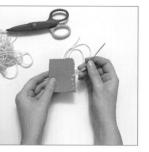

3 Cut the felt to make a folded oblong the length of one finger and twice the width. Sew two sides.

4 Turn the sewn felt inside-out to hide the stitching. Cut two small triangles for the ears.

5 Pinch together the corners of the long edge of the triangle and sew securely.

6 Sew the ears to the top of the sewn oblong. Cut out features in a contrasting felt and glue to the puppet.

▶ **WHAT TO DO**

· Ask each child to tell you about their toy: what is it called? Where do you keep it at home? What does your toy look like?
· Tell the children they are going to make their own finger-puppet toys.
· Follow steps one to six to make the finger puppets.

In our favourite box

Can speak clearly. Can listen when others are speaking

Can play imaginatively as part of a group

Keep the box in the home corner, so the children can continue with the activity during free-play time.

You could decorate a large cardboard box with coloured shiny paper if you don't have a treasure chest.

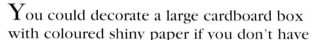
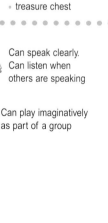

▶ **WHAT TO DO**

· Sit everyone on the floor around the treasure chest.
· Tell the children that the chest is special and it is full of favourite things to share.
· Tell them that your favourite thing to share is a bag of sweets. Take out a pretend bag of sweets and share them around.
· Ask the children to think of a favourite thing they could share with everyone.
· Let each child take turns pretending to take their favourite thing out of the chest and sharing it with the other children.

Resources

The resources section provides a useful range of material to supplement the activities in this book. The booklist below contains a selection of stories, information books, poems, and songs, and page 59 gives you room to add additional resource materials. Pages 60–61 are full of hints and tips on how to create an exciting wall display and you will find templates for many of the creative activities on pages 62–63. The index on page 64 lists every activity contained in All About Me.

Story books

'Alfie's Feet', Shirley Hughes. Picture Lions.
'An Evening at Alfie's', Shirley Hughes. Fontana Picture Lions.
'Angry Arthur', Hiawyn Oram. Red Fox.
'Avocado Baby', J. Burningham. Picture Lions.
'Can't You Sleep Little Bear?', Waddell and Barbara Firth. Walker Books.
'Dad's Back', Jan Omerod. Walker Books.
'Do You Dare?', Paul and Emma Rogers. Orchard Books.
'Doing the Washing', S. Garland. Bodley Head.
'Gran and Grandpa', Helen Oxenbury. Walker Books.
'I Feel Angry', Brian Moses and Mike Gordon. Wayland Publishers.
'I Feel Sad', Brian Moses and Mike Gordon. Wayland Publishers.
'I Like Books', Anthony Browne. Walker Books.
'I Like Me', N. Carlson. Picture Puffin.
'It's My birthday', H. Oxenbury. Walker Books.
'Jack and Jake', Aliki. Piccolo Books.
'Joe Can Count', Jan Omerod. Mulberry Books.
'Kingfisher Treasury of Nursery Stories', S. Price. Kingfisher.
'Moonlight', Jan Omerod. Picture Puffins.
'My Naughty Little Sister', D. Edwards. Methuen.
'Nandy's Bedtime', Errol Lloyd. Bodley Head.
'Nina at Carnival', Errol Lloyd. Bodley Head.
'Postman Pat's Foggy Day', John Cunliffe. Hippo Books.
'Something Special', Nicola Moon. Orchard Picture Books.
'So Much', Trish Cooke. Walker Books.
'Story Chest Get Ready Books', A. and B. Thomas Nelson and Sons Ltd.
'Titch', Pat Hutchins. Bodley Head.
'What will the weather be like today?', Paul Kazuko Roagers. Orchard Books.

'When Grandma Came', Jill Paton-Walsh and Sophy Williams. Puffin Books.
'You'll Soon Grow Into Them Titch', Pat Hutchins. Picture Puffins.
'10, 9, 8, Molly Bang', Picture Puffins.

Information books

'My Science Book of Light', Neil Ardley. Dorling Kindersley.
'My Body', B. Matthias and R. Thomson. Franklin Watts.
'All About You', C. and L. Anholt. Heinemann.
'I Have Two Homes', Althea. Dinosaur.
'How Do People Dress?' E. Urai. Macdonald.
'Taking Care with Strangers', K. Petty. Franklin Watts.
Be Safe Series: 'On The Road'. Franklin Watts.

Poetry

'Meet the Family' (Collection) S. Grindley. Orchard Books.
'Anger' from the Tinderbox Assembly Book, S. Barratt. A & C Black.
'Smile Please' (Collection) T. Bradman. Young Puffin.
'Nursery Rhymes', chosen by Ronne Randall. Ladybird.

Music

'How Many People Live in Your House?', 'I've Got a Body' and 'The Angry Song' from the Tinderbox Song Book. A & C Black
'She's the Best Mum in the World' from Sing a Song of Celebration. Holt Rinehart Winston
'When I am Happy', 'Caring for Myself' and 'Clothes' from Sing As You Grow. Ward Lock Educational
'How do you Feel Today?' from Songs from Play School. BBC

Notes

Note down additional resources on this page.

Creating a wall display

To make a high-quality wall display to accompany a topic theme takes time and experience. The display should reflect all the children's achievements and progress and the educational areas covered in the nursery. It should also provide a reference point for whole group discussion. In this display, for example you could point to the flags and say "Do you remember when we had our Italy Day?" A themed display also informs parents and visitors what the children are learning about, and places each finished product into a wider context. By following a few simple rules, even the less artistic among us can produce an exciting display.

Display hints and tips

- Take every opportunity to look at displays in other nurseries. Jot down ideas you see and use them in your own nursery.
- Agree among all staff how you will write each letter of the alphabet and numbers on displays. Stick to that style to achieve consistency.
- Make sure each child is represented in displays. Name and date all pieces of work.
- Change displays regularly. Set aside time for creating displays when you do your planning.
- Let children choose the content of the display and ask them to help you mount their work.
- Plan which work you will need to collect for display.
- Put up finished work/models/photographs as quickly as you can after the children have finished it. This shows that you value the children's efforts and makes them more likely to talk about the display because the content is still fresh in their minds.
- Make sure the display shows the educational achievement of each child. Displays should not be seen as a decoration to brighten up the nursery.
- Include 3-D and 2-D work, photographs, quotes, and annotated work showing adults' questions and children's comments, attitudes and approach. This places the finished product into context by informing parents and visitors about how a piece of work was achieved.
- Label each educational area on a display so that parents and visitors can see that in this nursery children are receiving a balanced early years curriculum.
- Keep displays tidy. If paper is ripped, fix it. This way, everybody learns to respect and look after other people's work.
- Use bright paper to cover a display board, make a border and for mounting work. Tawky paper is a good resource.
- If you create an interactive display, make sure each child is given time to use it.

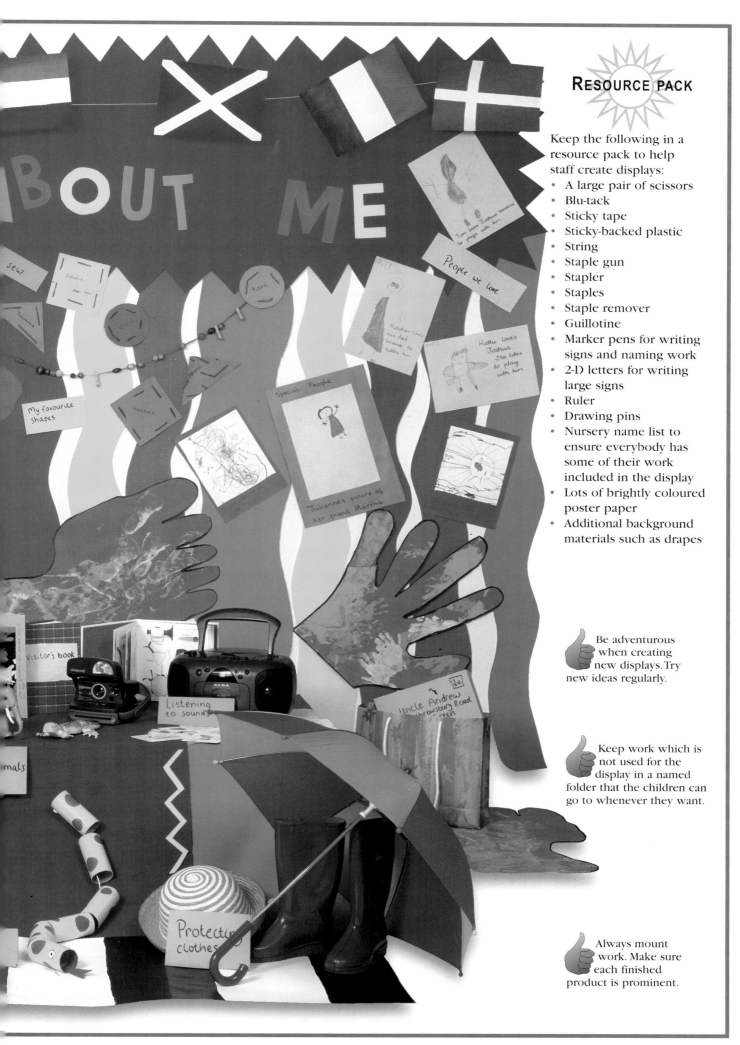

ABOUT ME

TEMPLATES

Cross face template for Puzzle
pictures (12) page 44

Surprised face template for Puzzle
pictures (12) page 44

Body template for Body part
puzzle (10) page 15

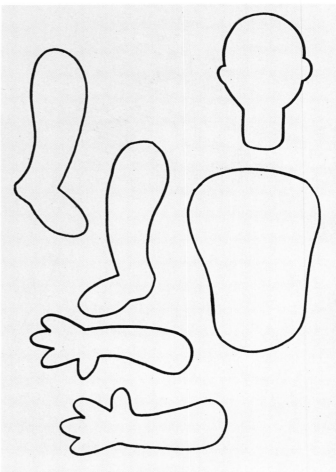

Shadow puppet template for Looking
at my shadow (9) page 15

Happy face template for Puzzle
pictures (12) page 44

Sad face template for Puzzle
pictures (12) page 44

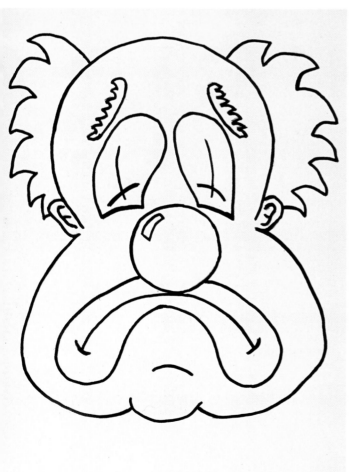

Sad clown face template for
Different moods (8) page 14

Happy clown face template for
Different moods (8) page 14

Index

Acknowledgments

Nursery World would like to thank:

Hope Educational for lending us many of
the props used in this book.
Production assistance: Jessica Tibbles
Editorial advice: Liz Roberts, Ruth Thomson

Digital artwork by Colin Bunner
Props made by Jim Copley
Illustrations by Jim Copley